DISCOVER

ZOMBIES

DO YOU BELIEVE?

This series features creatures that excite our minds. They're magic. They're myth. They're mystery. They're also not real. They live in our stories.

45TH PARALLEL PRESS

Published in the United States of America by Cherry Lake Publishing Group
Ann Arbor, Michigan
www.cherrylakepublishing.com

Reading Adviser: Beth Walker Gambro, MS Ed., Reading Consultant, Yorkville, IL
Book Design: Felicia Macheske

Photo Credits: © Prezoom.nl/Shutterstock.com, cover, 1; © leolintang/Shutterstock, 6; © all_about_people/
Shutterstock, 9; © Noska Photo/Shutterstock, 11; © Suzanne Tucker/Shutterstock, 13; © Raisa Kanareva/Shutterstock,
15; Jandrie Lombard/Shutterstock, 21

Graphic Elements Throughout: © denniro/Shutterstock; © Libellule/Shutterstock; © sociologas/Shutterstock;
© paprika/Shutterstock; © ilolab/Shutterstock; © Bruce Rolff/Shutterstock

45th Parallel Press is an imprint of Cherry Lake Publishing.

Library of Congress Cataloging-in-Publication Data

Names: Loh-Hagan, Virginia, author.
Title: Discover zombies : magic, myth and mystery express / Virginia Loh-Hagan.
Description: Ann Arbor, Michigan : Cherry Lake Publishing, 2023. | Series: Magic, myth, and mystery express |
    Audience: Grades 2-3 | Summary: "Are all zombies clumsy and slow? Do zombies ever attack alone? Books in the
    Magic, Myth, and Mystery Express series for young readers explore spooky creatures that go bump in the night,
    fill our dreams (or nightmares!), and make us afraid of the dark. Written with a high-interest level to appeal to a
    more mature audience and a lower level of complexity, clear visuals help struggling readers along. Considerate
    text includes fascinating information and wild facts to hold readers' interest and support comprehension.
    Includes table of contents, glossary with simplified pronunciations, and index"—Provided by publisher.
Identifiers: LCCN 2022039299 | ISBN 9781668919668 (hardcover) | ISBN 9781668920688 (paperback) |
    ISBN 9781668923344 (pdf) | ISBN 9781668922019 (ebook)
Subjects: LCSH: Zombies—Juvenile literature.
Classification: LCC GR581 .L63 2023 | DDC 398.21—dc23/eng/20220818
LC record available at https://lccn.loc.gov/2022039299

Cherry Lake Publishing would like to acknowledge the work of the Partnership for 21st Century Learning, a network
of Battelle for Kids. Please visit *http://www.battelleforkids.org/networks/p21* for more information.

Printed in the United States of America
Corporate Graphics

Dr. Virginia Loh-Hagan is an author, university professor, former classroom teacher, and
curriculum designer. She feels like a zombie every morning. She's a big fan of *The Walking Dead*.
She lives in San Diego with her very tall husband and very naughty dogs.

CONTENTS

CHAPTER ONE

Brain Eaters

Zombies eat brains. They **infect** others. Infect means to make sick. They turn humans into zombies.

Zombies are **undead** creatures. Zombies are dead. But they act alive. Zombies have **decomposing** bodies. Their bodies fall apart. Their skin slowly rots.

Did You KNOW?

Mummies are undead. But they're not zombies. Zombies are always decomposing. Mummies are preserved. They're saved from decomposing as quickly.

Zombies limp. They usually move slowly. They're clumsy. They moan. They groan.

There's no such thing as a lone zombie. Where there's one, there's more.

Explained by
SCIENCE

There are diseases that make people like zombies. One disease attacks cells. Skin rots off. The sick people can look like zombies.

Know the LINGO!

Cluster: a group of zombies in a small, confined area

Drone: the loud sound a horde makes

Grab zone: the area around a zombie in which a victim can be grabbed

There are different types of zombies. Walkers are the most common. They're regular zombies.

Runner zombies are the most dangerous. They can run. They're fast. They're new zombies.

All types of zombies are dangerous.

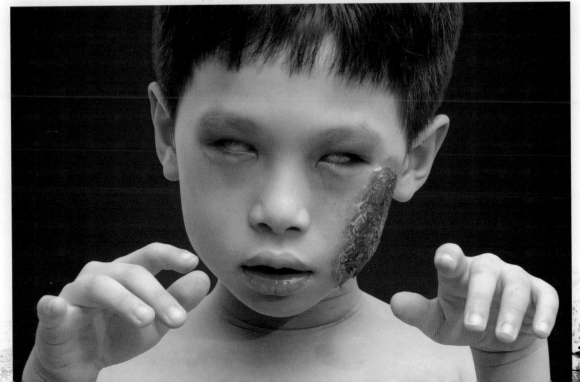

CHAPTER TWO

Beware of Zombies!

Zombies are scary. They're dead. But they still move. They bite. They attack. They eat humans.

Zombies tend to hang out where they used to live.

Have You HEARD?

Jewel wasps sting cockroaches. They put poison in the cockroaches' brains. They control their brains.

Zombies like noise. They go to the noise. They attack in **hordes**. Hordes are zombie groups.

Zombies aren't hurt by drugs, poisons, gases, electricity, or suffocation.

CHAPTER THREE
Zombie Weaknesses

Most zombies are slower than humans. It's easy to kill 1 zombie. But it's hard to kill a horde.

Zombies don't have superpowers. They have fewer abilities than when they were humans.

STAY SAFE!

- Feed salt to a zombie. This will make a zombie return to the grave.

- Get fit! Practice running. Lift weights. Learn to fight.

There are 3 ways to kill zombies. One, damage their brains.

Two, cut off their heads. Three, set them on fire. Fires kill zombies.

In a fight against vampires, zombies would lose.

CHAPTER FOUR

Becoming a Zombie

There are different ways to become a zombie. A person dies. Then the person becomes undead. The person becomes a zombie. A zombie can bite a person. The sickness spreads from the zombie to the person.

ORIGINS

Zombie stories started in West Africa. It started with **voodoo**. Voodoo is a religion. It uses folk magic.

Long ago, some people were buried alive. Doctors thought they were dead. But they weren't. Thieves dug up their graves. They wanted to steal jewelry.

But they got a surprise. The people in the graves were still alive! The thieves thought the dead had risen. These stories made zombies a part of our culture.

There is no cure. Once a person is bitten, that person is doomed.